Table of Contents

1

The Three P's of Success!

Starting and building an internet business is not an easy task. There is the never-ending learning about promotion, marketing, website design and building, technical problems, HTML, CGI, java; the list goes on and on. There are a few things you should think about when you are planning your online business. These three things are some of the most basic yet most important aspects that could make your business a success!

These are Perseverance, Passion and People!

Perseverance - Building a successful online business can take months or even years. Examine your goals and your life.

Will you have what it takes to not give up when things are going bad?

Do you have the determination to work this business for weeks or months without making any money?

Do you want to give up most of the small amount of spare time that you now have?

Go over these questions in your mind and see what you come up with. Despite all the "get rich quick" ads you see, this most likely will not happen. Most people will not even get rich slowly, however, you can make a good income.

You might start making a small amount of money in a few weeks or months, then you might not make any for a few months. You must not let yourself give up, when business is not all it s cracked up to be! You must have **Perseverance!**

Passion - When you are choosing your business, build your business around something that interests you, something that you are passionate about. This will help you keep going when things get tough.

Will I want to work with this business everyday?

Does this business interest me enough to keep my determination going?

Will my passion override any doubts that I will have about becoming successful?

Ask yourself these questions and see what the answers are. You cannot build a successful business around something you have no passion or knowledge about. If you are nuts about horses, build your business around horses, not cats! You must have **Passion!**

**People - When you are working an online business, you have to get involved with people. It may not be face to face, but you will have to deal with people from all over the world, everyday. Treat everyone with respect and answer all questions in a timely and courteous manner. You must also be able to deal with rude people. Treat these people with respect also. Be firm, but courteous. Rarely have I had to deal with this problem, but it does come up.

Do I want to have to deal with all those people on a day-to-day basis?

Can I handle all the different situations that can arise when dealing with people?

Can I accept the fact that I cannot please everyone and be able to handle the rejection?

You do not necessarily have to be "the life of the party" but you must be able to handle the problems that working with all kinds of people can bring. You must be able to deal with people!

I must tell you that I have made so many friends since starting online. It is one of the most enjoyable aspects of Internet marketing.

When I planned out Seymour Products, I really thought about what I wanted to do and how I wanted to do it. Because of that planning I have learned a few things about myself.

I have learned that I have more perseverance than I thought possible.

I have learned that I have a passion for helping people get started with their business and that I am good at it.

I have learned that working with people all over the world has been a thoroughly enjoyable, rewarding and interesting experience.

Remember the three P's of success when planning your goals and your chances of building a profitable business will be much greater!

#2

5 Powerful Article Writing Tips

Writing articles is one of the most powerful, if not the most powerful methods of building your reputation and your online business. Not only do you get unlimited exposure, but it is free as well!

If your article is well-written, you will probably get listed on numerous websites as well as in several ezines. This will establish you as someone who knows what they are talking about and will more than likely bring you many visitors and subscribers.

People will start to come to you when they need information or products or advice. This is a great way of establishing your online presence.

Writing articles is not as hard as you may think. You do not have to be a professional writer to produce an effective article. Below are some tips to help you get started.

1. Don't worry about big fancy words.

People are looking for easy to understand, down-to-earth articles to help them learn. They are not interested in being impressed with encyclopedia language skills.

2. Advertise in your resource box, not the article.

Do not use you article as a big sales letter for a product or program. Give your info in the resource box. I would recommend you just try to get people to sign up for your newsletter or free report/ecourse in your resource box. Save the selling for later.

3. Make yourself accessible if someone wants to get in touch with you.

People want to know that they can get in touch with you if they have questions about your article, website, etc. Always make it easy for them to find you.

4. Provide basic, real, useful information as well as resources to go along with the information.

When writing your article, try to list some useful resources that your readers can utilize along with the information you give them. This will further give people a reason to want to stay in touch with you or your website.

5. Write from the heart!

Do not be afraid to let your personality shine through in your writing. This will make people more apt to trust you and will also make them more comfortable. Write as if you were talking to a friend and let the real you shine through. I think people appreciate this more than trying to sound like something you are not!

Do not let your doubts stop you from writing articles to build your reputation and your business.   I did for awhile, but then took the plunge.

#3

8 Steps to Organizing Your Life & Business

Your life is a mess!
Your business is going nowhere!
Your house looks like a tornado hit it!

Does this sound familiar? Are you overwhelmed? Do you feel like your life and business are out of control and going nowhere?

Well, if you do, you are not alone. Believe me, we all get this feeling at one time or another - maybe more often. There ARE ways of taking control and getting organized!!

Step 1

STOP!! This is a very important step so do not take it lightly. You must stop and step back. Take some time and figure out exactly what you want and need to do to organize your life.

Step 2

Go to "your place" and bring a notebook and pen. We all have a place where we like to go to ponder, think, figure things out. If you do not have such a place, find one. Whether it be the beach, the bathtub, a quiet spot in the woods or at the park. We all need a place to clear our minds and sort things out once in awhile. You must be able to be alone for this task!

Step 3

Take a little time to clear your mind and free yourself from all the "stuff" of life. Then you can think clearly and objectively. When your mind is cleared, start thinking about what you want your life and your business to be. Write these thoughts down. These are your goals. In order to organize your life, you must know what your goals are.

Step 4

After you have determined your goals, you need to write down the steps to achieving these goals. Each major goal should be broken down into several smaller goals.

For example: If your goal is to build your business into a success, break this down into smaller more attainable goals such as:

Make website more effective.
Streamline ezine.
Research sales and target market.

Achieving one step at a time will build your confidence, which in turn will help you become more successful. After you get your plans written down, type them, print them and refer to them often. Do not let setbacks deter you. We all have them. Use them as a learning tool and a strength builder.

Step 5

Recruit your family! Yes, you can get your family to help in organizing your house which will also help in organizing the rest of your life. Hold a meeting and explain to your family what you AND them need to do. Assign each member certain chores and duties. Make sure they understand the importance of the task they are undertaking. This might take some time, but it will be very advantageous in the long run.

Step 6

Get started! The plans are made, the army is recruited, now is the time to put the plan into action! Each step will take time. Do not rush it or get discouraged if it doesn't happen overnight.

Step 7

Get rid of the clutter! If you have saved everything you ever got from emails to report cards - get rid of it. Keep only what you need to keep. Cleaning out the clutter will give you a feeling of control so you can take on the remaining steps more easily. It is a major step in getting organized!

Step 8

Do it again! Each day is another chance to get a little more organized and a step closer to achieving those goals! If you start feeling out of control and overwhelmed again, refer back to Step 1. Then get back into action! As each little step is accomplished, you will feel more in control and more confident. But even those of us who are in total control and meticulously organized, (is there such a person) will feel over-whelmed sometime. Consistency is the key. Once you get organized, stay organized.

Make organization and planning a daily habit. I don't think any of us are or can be completely organized all the time. But if we learn to take each step and day at a time, the times we are not organized or in control will be fewer are much farther between!!

#4

10 Easy Tips to Improve Your Ezine

Writing and publishing an ezine is a very important part of your online business so you want to make it the best possible ezine you can. I have made mistakes and changed and re-changed my ezine many times to make it the best it can be. I was still always looking for ways to improve MOE. Over the years I have learned a few simple ways to improve my ezine. You can easily implement these tips into your ezine.

1. ALWAYS, ALWAYS have your email, along with your name and url right at the top of your ezine. Unbelievably, I have read ezines where I could NOT find the email or even the name of the publisher!!! Also at the end of your ezine have name, address, phone number, and email and url again for easy access. Nothing is worse than trying to find contact info that for some reason is invisible!

2. Make sure you also always provide your subscribe and unsubscribe info as well. I would suggest putting this info at the bottom of the ezine. If you post your unsubscribe url right at the top of your ezine it is like you are inviting your subscribers to unsubscribe.

3. Provide a forum for your readers to interact with you and your other readers. A section entitled, Reader's Corner or Reader's Comments, where they can send in their comments, questions, feedback or whatever. This gives them a chance to become a part of the ezine.

This also helps build the reader-publisher relationship that is very important!

4. Keep your ezine clean and sharp looking. Don't add too many of the squiggles and decorations. They may look *cute* but they sometimes make it hard to read your ezine, thus prompting the ole' delete finger to become activated!

5. ALWAYS provide some original content. Writing articles is a great way of doing this. If you are not yet comfortable writing articles, (Yes, you can), write an editorial in each issue. Talk a bit about yourself, the latest happenings in the business, what is going on around the net, etc., things of that nature. This is a chance to bring out your personality, the main thing that makes your ezine unique!!

6. Having too many ads in each issue is a great way of bringing down the value of your ezine. I would suggest no more than 4 or 5 per issue. Reading an ezine that has 20 or 30 ads (oh yeah, I've seen them) is not very interesting or realistic. Most people would not even go through the whole thing. Here comes that delete finger again!! You want your advertisers to get more value for their money and having a limited number of ads is one of the best ways of doing this.

7. I think adding a small section for this 'n that is a good idea also. Some humor, a little fun, interesting tidbits, jokes, stories, etc. We are business men and women, but we don't have to be 100% business, 100% of the time!!

8. Privacy Policy - Put a privacy policy towards the top of the ezine. Let your readers know their privacy is safe with you and your ezine.

9. Proofread - Always proofread and double-check your text. You do not want your ezine to look like it was written by a 10 year old. Correct all spelling and grammatical errors.

10. Give your ezine an interesting and pulling name.
I have subscribed to most ezines just by the name alone. If the name gets my attention, I subscribe.

Names like:
Power Promotion Ezine
Marketing Mania Ezine
Web Success Ezine are short and to the point. They also make me want to read more.

Names like:

Internet Marketing News
John Doe's Ezine
Home Business News are more generic and do not get my attention!
They lack the "oomf" that make me want to subscribe.

I hope some of these tips give you an idea of how you can improve your
ezine and make it the best it can be. Remember that ezine publishing is
an important aspect of your online success. Good luck and success to
you all!!

#5

10 Power-Packed Promotion Strategies

There are many ways to creatively and affordably promote your online
business. I have tried all of the following and they worked very well for
me.

Joint Ventures - Participating in joint ventures with fellow publishers
can be a very profitable experience. This could be anything from a group
pop under window to advertising each other's ezines in your welcome
letter. I also know a lot of people have had some results with signature
buddies, where you would swap ads, so to speak, in each other's email
sigtag.

Writing Articles – Writing articles is an extremely effective method of building your reputation and your business. Writing articles is not hard. just stick with what you know and do not think you have to use big words to impress anyone. People are just looking for understandable articles with helpful info and useful resources. Write as if you were talking to a friend.

Ad Swaps - Swapping ads, or running another publisher's ad in exchange for him/her running yours, is a very popular method of promotion. There are hundreds of thousands of ezines on the net and most of the publishers are willing to swap ads. When writing to a fellow publisher, be sure to include a link to a sample issue of your ezine. Introduce yourself and let them know how you know about their ezine. Tell them about your ezine and suggest a possible swap. There are publishers who will even swap solo ads which is a great opportunity!

Discussion Lists - Participating in discussion groups can get you established as an expert in your field as well as build your reputation as one who is there when needed. This can bring you subscribers, customers and clients. Always follow each group's guidelines for posting and treat everyone with respect and courtesy.

Message Boards – Message boards are similar to discussion groups. Find a few quality boards and visit regularly. Participate and help whenever possible by offering your experience, advice, expertise or support. Always follow the rules.

Free Ecourses - Compile a series of articles and turn them into a mini ecourse. Give step by step info and provide helpful resources to compliment said info. Always provide links to your website, ezine and any products that are applicable. You also want to have your email on every page so it is very easy to contact you. Assemble your course on a free autoresponder and start offering it to your subs, visitors and submit it to fellow webmasters for distribution.

Free Ebooks - Creating an ebook is not hard. You can simply compile several articles that you or other people have written. Provide tips, resources and information. Offer your ebook to webmasters, ebook directories and ezine publishers for distribution.

Free Directories - There are hundreds of free ezine, business, and website directories all over the net. Take some time each day or week and submit your heart out! The more places you get listed, the more exposure you get.

Link Exchanges - Similar to ad swaps only you are listing other links on your website in exchange for your link being listed on their website. Set up a special set of pages with different categories for link exchanges.

AutoResponders - Autoresponders are used to mail out follow-ups to ezine subscribers, requests for more information, orders, article requests, etc. Effective follow-ups can raise your sales substantially.

If you consistently use some or all of these methods, your business is sure to grow. They have been very productive for me and can be for you as well.

#6

25 Easy Money-Saving Tips

1. Cut out the soda and drink more water! You'd be surprised how much you will save.

2. Go over your grocery list. Try buying more off-brands. Most of the ones I've tried are just as good as their more expensive counterparts.

3. Buy clothes and shoes for you and the kids from the clearance racks. I have been buying my sons' school clothes this way for years!

4. Get movies from the library instead of renting them.

5. Same with books, borrow instead of buy. We usually only read them once anyway.

6. Go on a picnic instead of going to the restaurant. It is more fun and much cheaper!

7. Toss all your change in a "piggy bank" of some kind and let it accumulate for a few months or longer. You will think you struck it rich! (Not really, but it does add up)

8. If you have all the movie channels, cut them down a bit. Most of the movies rotate through them all anyway.

9. Do your laundry at night. The rates are cheaper.

10. Give your clothes an extra spin as it costs less to run a washer than the dryer.

11. Ask your credit card companies for a lower interest rate. Sometimes rather than lose a good customer, they will grant your wish!

12. Buy your holiday decorations AFTER the holiday. You can save up to 75% or more.

13. Turn down your heat a couple degrees more at night and throw on an extra blanket.

14. Clean behind your refrigerator at least once a year to get out all the dust and dirt that can cost you more money.

15. Save empty bread bags and grocery bags instead of buying box after box of storage bags.

16. Keep your car tune and your tires properly inflated to save money on gas.

17. Buy inexpensive fabric for cloth napkins, doilies, etc.

18. Be creative when it comes to decorating. Use sheets to make curtains. Use an old quilt as a cozy wall-hanging. Create an artful display with family photos.

19. Save the new, convenient plastic coffee cans with handles. Paint them, decorate them and use them for organizers for kids' art supplies, your CDs, pens & pencils, food envelopes, recipes, craft supplies, etc.

20. Turn unused stuff into money. If you have a gift you haven't used or that shirt you bought and never wore, take them back to the store. You might not get full price, but some is better than none.

21. Use petroleum jelly to remove make-up. It is much more economical then beauty products made for removing make-up.

22. Hydrogen peroxide can be used to kill germs in cuts and sores rather then expensive antibiotic medicines.

23. Make windowsill or container gardens and grow herbs and fresh vegetables.

24. Instead of a night on the town, send the kids to Grandma's and have a romantic night at home.

25. Make and STICK TO a budget!

I hope some of these tips help you as they have helped us.

#7

35 Tips for Online Success

1. Don't overload your site with flashing lights and slow loading graphics. Keep it simple and to the point.

2. Put a little of yourself into your site and make it unique.

3. Have your contact information listed on every page.

4. Make every page of your site consistent. You want your site to be easy to understand and navigate.

5. Provide a lot of useful content and resources. Don't just make your site one big ad.

6. Make yourself available to answer questions and to help your visitors when needed.

7. Answer all email inquiries in a timely and courteous manner.

8. Make it very easy for people to order your products. The easier to order, the more orders you'll get.

9. Publish an ezine. This will enable you to keep in contact with your readers and form a very important relationship.

10. Use an autoresponder for follow-ups.

11. Write and submit articles for publication in other ezines.

12. Participate in ad swaps with other publishers.

13. Set up a links page and exchange links with other websites.

14. Build your reputation and yourself as a foundation for your online success.

15. Follow-up on all sales and inquiries.

16. Develop contacts and relationships with other publishers and netpreneurs.

17. Learn how to write your own ebook to sell or give away.

18. Join discussion lists and message boards and network, network, and network. Enjoy some new friendships along the way.

19. Find and join some good affiliate programs to help you learn marketing and selling and to add to your income.

20. Do not spam! If you are unsure if something is spam, find out before you proceed.

21. Purchase your own domain name.

22. List your ezine in several popular directories.

23. Be true to yourself and your customers. This will establish trust which is essential to your success.

24. Include some original material in your ezine. If you are not yet writing articles, write an editorial for each issue. Let your readers get to know you.

25. Do not insult other people. ALWAYS treat others with respect.

26. Subscribe to several popular ezines. Read and learn from them. The good ezines are loaded with information and resources.

27. Participate in joint ventures with ebook authors, ezine publishers, etc. This is a good way of making more money and providing resources for your subscribers. Always review the product before you promote it.

28. Never stop learning!!   There is an endless amount of information to learn when running an online business. Do not ever think that you know all you need to know.

29. Be open to new ideas and be willing to take risks.

30. Learn from others who have been there already. Most of the publishers and netpreneurs are willing and happy to help newbies.

31. When publishing an ezine, stuff it with useful content and resources. Give your readers what they crave - information! Don't throw 30 ads together and call it an ezine!

32. Thoroughly check out all opportunities and offers before joining or buying. There are a lot of scammers out there.

33. When writing articles, write as if you are teaching. Don't turn the article into a sales letter for one of your products.

34. Back up all your information and work, so you do not lose it. This is very important!

35. Do not think you have to read, buy or use every product, ebook or program out there.

36. Choose a business that will bring out your passion and commitment. Running an online business can be a very rewarding and fulfilling experience.

I wish you all the success and satisfaction with your online venture. Do not let the frustration or setbacks get you down. Use them as a learning experience to make you stronger, better and more successful!

#8

Create a Library of Articles for Automatic Promotion

Writing articles and submitting them for publication is a very powerful promotion tactic. BUT, this can be taken a step further to put your articles on auto-pilot.

First of all, you need to get a good free autoresponder

Each time you write an article, what you want to do is autoresponder account for that article. For example, probably have an account named articlelibrary@getre you want to do is put the article and a short but court note in the message.

To tie your library together, you want to make one message that contains all your article titles along with each autoresponder address. This account would be named allarticles or article-index or something on that order, whatever you want. ;-)

This way, people can request all your articles or just certain ones they might be interested in.

You can also give this list of articles and autoresponder addresses their own page on your website. This will give your articles additional exposure.

Then to help spread the word about your article library, add a link to your sigtag, mention it on discussion lists when someone asks for articles, put it in your resource box, mention it in your ezine, etc.

Your articles will automatically be giving you free exposure while you can concentrate on other aspects of your business!

And remember, you do not have to be an "expert" writer to write effective and helpful articles. Do not let your own self-doubt stop you from this excellent method of building your business.

Just write what you know and give the readers basic and straight-forward information and resources. And let your personality shine through in your articles, so your readers feel they know you and can trust you.

Ok, so get started and write that first article! ;-)

#9

Start an Article Trading Center

A great way to improve your search engine ranking and attract more visitors to your site would be an **Article Trading Center**. This is where you would swap articles with other webmasters/article authors in order to benefit both parties. This is done much the same way as exchanging links but with far more effective results (in my opinion). There are many benefits to adding an article center to your site:

*Adds content to your website
*Builds your reputation and online presence
*Provides readily available ezine content
*Improves your search engine status
*Establishes you as a reliable online presence
*Increases your circle of contacts and networking

What you need to do is trade articles with quality, websites that compliment, not compete, with your website. Join some of the article lists to find the type of article you are looking for. You can also visit websites with article directories.

When you find the articles you are looking for, contact the author and explain your offer. Let him/her know the benefits of trading articles with you. Be selective in choosing the articles. You want well-written articles that contain helpful information and/or resources.

Compiling a vast and varied Article Center will draw more visitors to your site as well as improve your ranks in the search engines. Having your articles posted all over the net will help build your reputation and increase your online success. Get started today on your new **Article Trading Center!**

#10

Let's Get Back to Business!

Well folks, now that we all had a nice holiday season, it is time to get back to business. Some things you can do to give your business a lift and charge into the new year are:

Reassess your goals - if you have previously written down your goals, go over them to see if how you have done. Have you achieved your goals? If not, you will need to try to figure out why and make some changes.

If so, what will your new goals be? Remember to use your goals as a guideline - they do not have to be etched in stone.

Expand your networking - You now have a very well established circle of contacts, but you always need to be networking and meeting new contacts. Get to know others, learn from them, let them learn from you and get to know you. This is an excellent way of building a strong foundation for your business.

Streamline your business plan - Review your plans for your business. As with your goals, you probably need to upgrade.

Revamp your website - Look over your website and see how you can give it a breath of fresh air for the new year. You don't need to change the entire design - some new colors or graphics, or some minor rearranging could do the trick. Also, adding more content is always a wise decision.

Raise your search engine ratings - Tweak your keywords and refine your content to match. Search engines take no crap so make your site the best it can be for those spiders!

Tweak your ezine/blog - Review your ezine, the layout, design, and content. Maybe add a new section or add some reader interaction. Ask your subscribers what they would like to see in your ezine and what they don't like about it. This is a great way to find out what would improve your ezine/blog.

Refine your marketing plan - Do some research. You need to keep up with the latest trends and changes in the online marketing world. You may need to make some major changes in the way you market your business.

Strengthen your reputation - Go the extra mile for your customers/subscribers. Show them that you deserve their trust and respect. Build a reputation stronger then the Great Wall of China!

Strive to learn more - There is so much to learn in this business and the more we know, the more we can do. So, let's make a point to learn all we can!

Learn how to work smarter, not harder! I'm ready, are you? OK, let's make this year more successful than ever!

#11

The Basics of Starting an Online Business

If you are looking to start your own online business, the first step is to decide what type of business you want to get into. You need to choose something that you are interested in and like to do. If the passion is not there, you will more than likely not succeed!

Ask yourself these questions:

Can I dedicate myself to this business?

Contrary to what a lot of ads tell you, there is no get rich quick business. If you start an online business, you will be putting in hours each day to make that business successful. You will need to be very dedicated to that business to succeed. Weeks, months, or even years could go by before you start making any money. Make sure you are ready for that kind of commitment before you start your business.

What do I want to accomplish with this business?

Make sure you know exactly what you want to do with your business. Write out your business plans and goals. This will help you to realize what you want to do with your business and how you want to do it.

After you decide on a business, get your goals in order and make the commitment, the next step is to build a website or get one built for you. If you decide to build one yourself, there are tons of resources to help you learn how:

Building and maintaining a website is a constant learning process. You need to keep up with ever changing information.

You will also need a domain, which will be the name of your site and business. For example: if you are selling business/office supplies, try to find a name that really zeros in on what you offer, like –
Affordable Office Supplies or Business Supplies and More.

This would be the link and main page to your website.

Once you get all this set up you are ready to start networking, promoting, advertising, marketing, etc. This is what takes the time and commitment. You cannot build a website and sit back and wait for the clients/customers to find you. You have to go out and find your customers.

There are several methods of promoting and networking online. Remember to advertise and promote your business offline as well.

Online Promotion:
ad swaps
ezine publishing
forum networking
joint ventures
ezine advertising

directory submissions
link exchanges
contests and many more!

Offline Promotion:
flyers
bulletin boards
freebies (such as ink pens)
business cards
newspapers
radio stations and many more!

#12

Budgeting Made Easy

I am a strong believer in budgeting because even with the smallest of incomes, it can help you make your money go farther. Budgeting is not hard and you do not need a degree in mathematics to be able to do it. You also do not need expensive software or online programs to write an effective budget.

First thing you need to do is make a list of all your bills and expenses - monthly, weekly, quarterly, etc. I do my budget by the week because we get a weekly paycheck. Some people would do a monthly or bi-weekly budget. For the example, I will do a weekly budget.

So here is an example of a list of expenses:

Mortgage $250
Groceries $300
Heat $50
Phone $75
Electric $80
Internet $20
Cable $50
Insurance $60
Car Payment $200
Credit Cards $25, $75 and $100
Gas for car $100

Now to start your budget, you would put each bill a week or two before it is due. For example, if your mortgage is due on the 10th of the month, you would either have it paid the last week of the month before or the first week of the month.

Example budget using example bills listed above with a income of $450 a week.

March 5
Internet $20
Groceries $75
Gas $25
Credit Cards $125
Insurance $60

Total $305

March 12
Car Payment $200
Cable $50
Groceries $75
Gas $25

Total $350

March 19
Mortgage $250
Groceries $75
Gas $25

Total $350

March 26
Groceries $75
Gas $25
Credit Card $75
Heat $50
Phone $75
Electric $80

Total $380

Now this is your very basic and simple budget. You would want to add in things like Christmas, birthdays, taxes, etc. when appropriate. With a tight budget, you would try to add those in when you have an extra payday. These come every third month, I do believe.

What you have left is for whatever you choose to so with it. I would recommend that you add a weekly amount for savings/investments to help with the future.

Also, if you want to do a budget for your business, I would suggest doing that separately.

I simply write my budget in a notebook and go over it every week when I write out the bills. I also then write out my grocery list for the weekly shopping.

I keep my budget, bills, monthly statements and such in a folder type binder. Each month when I pay a bill, I throw out the old statement and keep the new. This helps me keep track of things also.

Yes, sometimes it is hard to stick to a budget, but if you don't things could get much harder and the bills could start stacking up.

Budgeting might sound complicated, but when you use a simple method, it gets easy very quickly. You do not need to be an accountant or to have a expensive software program to help you do your budgeting. A simple notebook of paper and an ink pen or pencil is all you need. Oh, and a calculator to speed things up a bit. ;-) Happy Budgeting!!!

#13

Are You a Chicken Without Its Head?

Have you ever heard the expression, "Running around like a chicken with its head cut off!" Now, when I was a kid, we used to kill our own chickens and I know firsthand exactly what this means! ;-)

Do you jump from one place or project to another and feel like you are never getting anything done? Do you rush through each day like a freight train trying to get all your work done? Family, home, business, work.........does it ever end!!??!!

Life for most of us is pretty fast-paced and this can lead to problems both physically, and emotionally. What you need to do is "work smarter, not harder." I know we have all heard that one before and it is most definitely "easier said than done!" I am just full of them today, I guess! lol

One thing you need to do is make out a schedule (with room for a little flexibility) that will be used as a guideline. Don't make the mistake of writing out an extremely tight schedule and then "frying your brains," trying to stick to it. Not being able to follow your schedule can be frustrating to say the least, but preparing a flexible schedule makes it less stressful on you and everyone else.

You should also have a "to do list" for each day. Write down the most important things that HAVE to get done that day, followed by the things that should get done that day and then things that have time or are a continuing effort.

For example:

Monday To Do List
Must Do - Write ezines, answer important email
Try To Do - Add more resources to site, arrange ad swaps
Continuing - Submit to directories

I always have a list like this right next to me on my desk so I know what needs to be done each day.

You also need to take some time for yourself. I have a hard time with this one and I am sure many others do as well. You feel like you just don't have the time to give yourself this luxury. But think of it this way, if you take this time for yourself, you will be much more relaxed and refreshed to get "more work done in less time!"

What you can also do to help get things done is delegate the household chores. Give the kids each a few of the everyday chores. This helps a lot! They might gripe and groan, but it is good for them.

Working at home to me is a blessing, but it sometimes can be very hard to keep everything (including yourself) going.

You MUST have some kind of schedule and you MUST take some time for yourself as well as your family! If you do not, your business will suffer and so will your family!

DO NOT feel guilty about stealing 30-60 minutes a day just for you. YOU deserve it and your family would probably agree!

#14

10 Ways to DeClutter Your Home

Over time our homes, especially if they are smaller homes, have a tendency to accumulate and collect all kinds of treasures, gems and keepsakes, otherwise referred to as "junk".   ;-) Now we all know that one person's trash is another person's treasures, but our homes can only hold so much!!!

I have listed below several ways of going about the process of decluttering or decontamination, whichever term you prefer. ;-)

Of course, this process will not be done in one day, after all it took years (or if we are really good, months) to make it this way.

Start slow and take the time needed to follow through.
You will find that decluttering is not as hard as you thought it would be.

1. Cupboards - Go through all you kitchen cupboards, one at a time of course, and you will be amazed at what you find that can be thrown out. When I cleaned mine out not too long ago, I had four coffee maker decanters, that I could not even use anymore because I had a different coffee maker!   I also found spices that were about 10 years old!!

2. Bedroom Closets- The saying goes - If you haven't worn it or used it in a year, get rid of it. I am not sure I agree with that statement totally, but it is a good guideline to follow. I am always amazed at the clothes I get rid of (and how many I still have) when I clean out my closets!

3. Bookcases - Now, I don't know about you, but I have a tendency to gather books. At last count, I had well over 200 and definitely had to get rid of some of them. I looked them all over and got rid of the ones that didn't sound interesting. Also, go through knickknacks, papers, magazines, or anything else filling up those bookcases.

4. Kids Room - This is something that needs to be done about twice a year in my house. My boys go through their clothes, toys, video games, etc and out goes anything they are no longer interested in.

5. Bathroom - We know how cluttered and overflowing those vanities and medicine chests can get. Go through all those goodies and if it has hardened, softened or changed color, get rid of it! ;-)

6. Linen Closet - Towels, sheets, curtains, etc, are also things that need to be periodically sorted and tossed. I just recently discovered that we had almost 100 towels! Who knew?? I removed all the semi worn out ones and was left with about 30 or so. That should suffice.

7. Under Your Bed - This part of the decluttering can be quite scary. Proceed with caution and always have a weapon, such as broom, vacuum cleaner or bug spray with you! Who the heck knows what you will find under there, but I can bet a lot of it can go. ;-)

8. Organize - There are so many great products these days that hold everything. Get some inexpensive plastic boxes and neatly store all your items that are not in display or not used daily. You can get small ones in the dollar stores to organize your CDs, use them in your pantry or cupboards, store odd and ends, letters, papers, you name it!

9. Throw Out the Old - One thing you must absolutely remember when decluttering is you have to THROW AWAY the NOT USED or NOT WANTED. DO NOT just take everything out and rearrange!!! That is a temporary solution and is not sufficient!!!!!

10. Everything in its Place - Once you have everything decluttered and organized, get everyone to keep everything in its place and your home will remain organized and clutter free forever! Yea, right -nice dream, but we will be doing this very same thing in the not too distant future! ;-)

We have a fairly small home, so I go through this process about once a year. Decluttering and organizing gives me a sense of control and achievement. This might not mean much to some folks, but think a moment......... if you can get control over this part of your life, maybe taking control of the big things will not be so hard!   ;-)

#15

Quick & Easy Decorating Ideas

1. Make your house come "alive" with silk flowers, plants and trees.   Fill a pretty glass vase for a colorful centerpiece or fill an empty corner with a rustic birch tree.

2. In my kitchen as an alternative to expensive wallpaper borders, I use inexpensive grapevine garlands. I used four garlands and ran them all along the top of the walls.   Quick, easy, inexpensive and the effect is great!

3. For an inexpensive wall grouping, find a calendar with beautiful scenic pics or flowers or animals, whatever fits your decor.   Put 4, 6 ,8 or more of these pics in some nice frames and group them together on a wall. The effect is surprisingly pretty!

4. Find some colored bottles, jars, etc. you might have lying around or scout garage sales.   Fill these bottles with polished stones, colored

beads, seashells, or anything else you like and arrange them on a table or shelf.   Use different shapes and sizes for a more dramatic effect.

5. Go wild with baskets. Baskets come in many sizes, styles and colors and can be used for extra storage in any room. Use them in the bathroom for cosmetics, toiletries, towels, etc. In the kitchen they can hold utensils, recipes, or food items. Try them for magazines, books, or movies in the living room or bedroom. In the kids' room they make great places for toys, books, video games. The possibilities are endless!

6. One thing I would recommend for any home is candles. Candles are an inexpensive way to lighten, brighten and enhance any room in your home. Candles come in a variety of colors, shapes, sizes and scents. You can create a cozy, relaxing mood or you can spice it up and energize your mind and soul. Candles are much more than a decoration!

7. Arrange a grouping of family photos on a table or wall. This is one of the best ways to warm your home. Use frames in different sizes and styles to make the grouping more unique and interesting.

8. For organization, buy plastic storage tubs/boxes in pretty colors. Use them to store and organize your linen, toys, off-season clothes, memoirs, etc. Stack them in a corner for a pretty look.

9. Decorate an old wooden bench or trunk. Put a decorative pillow or cushion on it and place it by a window for an instant window seat!

10. Use your imagination! Anything and everything can be used for home decorating if you are creative with it!

#16

E-books are for E-veryone!

One of the best ways to build your online income is by writing & distributing ebooks. Ebooks can be a very effective tool for marketing your business and they can also be big money makers. Ebooks are also a useful resource for whatever information you are looking for.

There are a few things you should remember if you are going to write an ebook.

1. Just as your ezine should not be a giant ad, nor should your ebook. Be sure to fill it full of useful and valuable information.

2. Your ebook should be compiled in a simple, yet professional design. Make your ebook look good, but do not overdo. Make sure people can maneuver around the book with ease.

3. Take the time to do the research and write an effective and informative ebook. Your ebook will be circulating around the web and will say a great deal about you and your business.

4. Ebooks are a great giveaway for your visitors and/or subscribers. Everyone is looking for useful information which can be found in ebooks.

5. You should always use your first ebook as a giveaway. This will entice more people to read your ebook, which in turn will get more people to see how good it is. When you do write your first ebook to sell, you will have already established your reputation for writing a useful and informative ebook.

6. You do not have to be a writer to write an ebook. Just as with articles, all you need to do is gather, organize and outline your information. Always add resources and links when applicable. A good ebook for giveaway can be as simple as a collection of your articles or the articles of other authors.

7. After you finish your ebook, you want to start promoting it. Add it to your website, put it in your email sigtag, submit it to as many websites and directories that you can find, add it to your article resource box, announce it on message boards and email discussion lists where allowed, make a separate web page for it and submit the page to search

engines, add it to your ezine welcome letter as a free bonus. The possibilities are endless if you use your imagination and let as many people know about your ebook as possible. Be sure to encourage people to also give it to their subscribers/visitors as a free gift.

8. Make sure you have contact links listed in your ebook so people can easily contact you or visit your website. Also, be sure to have your ezine and subscribe address listed.

9. Everyone can find ebooks useful not only for finding the information they seek, but for promoting their business and website as well as establishing a solid reputation. They are also big moneymakers and just about anyone can write and profit from a carefully and effectively done ebook.

#17

Go Offline and Increase Your Traffic

Having an online business entails never ending online promotion, but do not forget to promote offline as well. There are many ways to spread the word offline about your business. Try a few of these affordable and easy ideas. These ideas are simple, yet can bring your site many visitors.

Flyers - Design and print flyers right from your computer. Post them on bulletin boards at grocery stores, churches, malls, post offices, banks, etc. Use brightly colored paper to get people's attention. Make the message interesting enough so they want to visit your site.

WebDecals - Purchase a WebDecal for your car. Promote while running errands, shopping or wherever you have to go. They are easy to use and inexpensive.

Local Papers - Run your ads in local newspapers. You can usually get these at very reasonable rates. Ask your local paper if they would consider doing a story about your business. Local papers frequently do a write up for local business owners.

Business Cards - Always have business cards on hand. Stick one in your monthly bills when you mail them out, leave one on the table with the tip when you leave the restaurant, stick them on bulletin boards, leave one whenever the opportunity arises.

Letterheads - You should have your url and logo on all printed materials that leave your home/office. Have your url stamped on all envelopes and letters and anything else you mail out.

Coupons - Print out coupons that offer discounts or freebies for anyone who visits your site from that coupon. Post these on bulletin boards, put them in all your outgoing mail, etc.

Freebies - Offer freebies from your site that have your url printed on them, such as ink pens, coffee mugs, matchbooks, calendars, etc. Lots of these items get seen by many people.

There are tons of ways to promote your online business offline. Expand on the ideas I have listed and really use your creative imagination. Bring more traffic to your site by going offline!

#18

You CAN Be a Great Salesperson!

When you are in sales, you have the choice to be successful or unsuccessful. The only one to set limits on your income and success is you! A career in sales is a challenge. Use that challenge to motivate and excite you. Meet and beat that challenge!

There are five basic components to sales:
prospecting
making contacts
qualification
handling objections effectively
closing

Do not fall into the "natural-born salesman" myth. A lot of people feel if they do not take to these components naturally they won't be able to at all. Forget this myth! You can learn to be a great salesperson - the choice is yours!

A sale is a learning experience. You need to be always learning and reviewing. A very effective method of learning is repetition. Write it, read it, speak it, hear it, and learn it !!

Characteristics of a successful salesperson:

1. Appearance - make the most of your unique individuality and walk into a room with pride and a commanding presence. Take pride in your selling career and in yourself.

2. Confidence - You need to "glow" with a sense of self-confidence. Even if you are not the best in sales YET, you can be. Let this feeling of confidence show through to everyone you talk to.

3. Overcoming fear - Know your fear so you can face it and overcome it! Once you do this, the confidence will shine through.

4. Enthusiasm - In sales, sometimes you will get the sale and sometimes not. That is to be expected. The trick is to stay enthusiastic even when you do not get the sale. Do not let it bring you down. Keep that enthusiasm going for the next prospect!

5. Desire - You have to have the desire to succeed. If you have the desire, you can overcome any obstacle and become a success!

6. Do not take rejection personally - In sales, there will be rejections. Do not let these rejections cause you to doubt yourself. Let them make you stronger and more enthusiastic for the next sale.

7. Caring and warmth - You need to actually care about your prospect and feel right about closing the sale. DO not try to bully people into buying. Lead them smoothly into a closing that will benefit them.

8. Continuing education - You need to always be learning. Invest some time and money into your mind and learn how to be the best salesperson you can be!

Great salespeople are not born great. They have the desire to become great. They take the time and invest in themselves and learn how to become great!

#19

Thrifty Decorating Ideas for the Holidays

Decorating for the holidays is a fun and exciting way to bring the holiday cheer to your home.   But, it can also be very expensive. Over the years, I have used many of the ideas below to save money and spruce up my holiday decor.

Halloween

Use tin cans for eerie jack-o-lantern luminaries. Before you throw those cans away, make more use of them. Poke holes in them in a scary face design and then use tealights or votive candles for lighting.   These are great for indoors or out.

Paint empty coffee cans to look like witches, goblins, ghosts, pumpkins. They look adorable and are great for holding, snacks, treats, etc.

Use pieces of plywood to make scary headstones for your yard!

Thanksgiving

Make a beautiful Thanksgiving centerpiece, with a pretty birch log. Drill holes in the log for autumn leaves/branches, birds. Be creative and add what you like. This is a great idea for a Christmas one as well. You could also use a pumpkin for a pretty Thanksgiving or Halloween centerpiece.

Fill baskets with leaves, mini pumpkins, gourds, acorns, and other natural autumn items.

Paint some tin cans to look like pilgrims, pumpkins, or scarecrows.

Christmas

Evergreen boughs! These can be used for centerpieces, mantle displays, arranged around candles, displayed on your wall with bulbs and other items. Add some pine cones, silk poinsettias, birds, etc. as well.

One of my favorite decorations is a pretty glass bowl or basket filled with colorful glass balls, pine cones, and little evergreen boughs. This makes a wonderful centerpiece or coffee table display.

Make a pretty potpourri basket filled with pine cones, evergreen sprigs, and dried oranges/apples.

Decorate empty canning jars and turn them into Christmas lanterns with votive candles.

Decorate your dining room chairs with pretty ribbon.

Turn old cds into mini-wreaths for your tree. Glue small pine cones, glitter, cotton (for snow), evergreen boughs, ribbon, stars, tiny glass balls.........the possibilities are endless. You have never seen all those free CD's put to such good use and what a fun project for the whole family!

Look around your house and use your imagination. Almost everything can be turned into a pretty decoration with a little creativity and work. ;-)

#20

Tips for Your Home Business

1. Get biz cards made up and have them with you always. Leave them at restaurants, send them with your monthly bills, post them on bulletin boards, hand them out to people you talk to. Always be aware of opportunity.

2. Along the same lines, always have catalogs or brochures in your car. You never know when someone might ask to see your products.

3. Do not forget to label all catalogs, brochures, order blanks, etc with your company name and address and URL (if applicable). You can either stamp them on or make your own labels. You can get inexpensive adhesive labels from Wal-Mart or other stores as well.

4. Get out there and get yourself and your product known. Talk about your products as much as you can to as many people as you can. Make it a part of your daily routine. Make your new business a part of every single day. Always be watching for opportunities. They are everywhere!

6. It helps also to have some sample items available so people can see the quality of the products. This can increase your orders.

7. Keep track of everyone who you give catalogs to or who orders from you to start building your mailing list. Get addresses and email addresses if possible to build your list. Stay in touch with these people and go the extra mile for your customers or potential customers.

8. Online marketing is great, but should be used in conjunction with other marketing methods such as flea markets, catalog distribution, home parties, mail order or others.

9. Study, research, and learn marketing techniques, how to sell, advertising ideas and tips.

10. Print out flyers and mail them out to local stores and shops. Let them know what you are offering and give your phone number. Flyers can be passed out in parking lots as well. Make sure you have permission.

11. Contact radio stations and offer your products as prizes for contests for some great exposure.

12. Talk to schools, churches, and other organizations that might be interested in using your products for fundraisers.

13. Have your catalogs and biz cards with you at kids' sports events. You could easily get orders just by arousing interest in your catalogs.

14. There are so many things you can do. Every time you get or hear of an idea that interests you, write it down in your planner or notebook. Organize your marketing and advertising efforts and ideas.

15. Local Papers - Run your ads in local newspapers. You can usually get these at very reasonable rates. Ask your local paper if they would consider doing a story about your business. Local papers frequently do a write up for local business owners.

Building a home business takes time and effort and then some, but do not give up. Have passion for your business and for your customers. You can succeed!

#21

Are You Suffering from Information Overload?

I have had several emails lately with people asking what to do about Information Overload. They spend all their time downloading free ebooks, subscribing and then deleting ezines, visiting websites and so on.

Well, let me tell you, I think we all go through that when we first come online. I know I had about 100 ebooks on my desktop along with reports, ecourses, and anything else that was offered for free. I had also subscribed to just about every ezine I could find and didn't have time to read any of them.

I finally realized that I was never going to read the ebooks, or all the ezines or any of the other freebies I had so carefully saved and foldered on my desktop.

So what I did was come to the point where I got rid of all but one or two of the ebooks, unsubbed from most of the ezines and got rid of all the reports, etc.

What you need to do is focus and get in control by cleaning out the clutter. Concentrate on you and your business and stay focused and in control.

You DO NOT need every ebook/program/report that comes down the pike to learn how to build an online business!

1. Go through all the ebooks and just throw them in the recycle bin. You will never be able to read or use all of them. If you happen to find a free ebook that actually has useful and helpful info, then by all means hang onto it and read it when you can.

2. Next go through all the ezines you are subbed to. Pick out a few that you really enjoy and actually find useful information and resources in.

3. Reports, ecourses, and such are generally nothing but lead-ins for you to buy their product. There are, of course, some good ones out there, but get rid of the sales pitches.

4. Try not to go through every website on the net. Find a few that really are useful and that have a webmaster that actually responds to your questions and earns your trust.

5. Find a few good discussion groups and message boards and learn from others who have been through the same thing. This is a good way to start networking and making new contacts.

6. Talk to some more experienced online business owners and stick with the ones who actually show an interest in you and your questions and do their best to help you.

7. Don't think you have to order every ebook, ecourse, program, etc from all the self-proclaimed Gurus out there. Most of the "Secret of Success" type products are nothing but a lot of well disguised hype. I have talked to some people who have purchased just about every "make money fast" product out there and have done nothing but "spend money fast".

I have been online for several years and have found that most free information is really nothing more than a big sales pitch. You will find that the best way to learn online is by doing and learning through your experiences and yes, mistakes.

Don't get me wrong. There are plenty of very helpful and dependable people out there that produce quality ezines, ebooks and programs. I know plenty of them.

The trick is to learn to sift through all the "crap" to get to the Gold! And you will. How do I know, you say? I know because I did plenty of sifting and learning through experience and by getting help from some very wonderful folks out there and you will too. ;-)

#22

How to Work at Home and Keep Your Sanity!

Working at home can be a blessing and/or a disaster depending on how you are able to handle it. A home business or job is not for all of us.   I know a lot of people who much prefer to "get out in the world" to work.

I absolutely love working at home. I did enjoy working outside the home as well, but I am a homebody and much prefer working at home.   It does have disadvantages and problems though as well.

* Isolation - This can be a tough one to deal with for some people. Sitting in your lonely little corner or home office hour after hour can get you down. When you start feeling isolated and lonely, contact an online friend and chat awhile. If no one is available, take a break and get outside. Take a walk to visit a friend or family member.   Just getting out in the fresh air can make you feel rejuvenated and alive again. Even a phone call to an old friend or your spouse, if possible, can do wonders.

* Self-discipline - This one can be a tuffy. Having your own business can tend to make us lazy once in awhile. I know it does me. ;-)   What I do, is go over my goals and the reasons I started my business in the first place. I also think about all my readers/customers who are counting on me. This helps me get back into focus and to get motivated to go back to work. You need to train yourself to work when it is work time because you have no boss to do it for you.

*Schedule Keeping - Making up a schedule is easy, sticking to it is not. I try not to have too strict of a schedule because it probably will need to be changed now and then. Try a daily schedule instead of a hourly one. This will make it much easier to bend it when you need to. Not being able to follow your schedule can be frustrating to say the least, but preparing a flexible schedule makes it less stressful on you and everyone else.

*Family Distractions - This is one of the main reasons it is so hard to stick to our schedules! ;-) Make time for your family and make sure they understand that work time is for work and family time is for them. With me, my family comes first and I arrange my schedule around them and it works out very well.

*Lack of Respect - Although we know how important our business is, our family or friends may not. They think we are playing around or just doing a hobby. You need to sit them down and explain that this is your job and it is very important to you and they need to respect that.   Be firm. They will get the message. ;-)

*Organization - Although we might be very organized, we just might not have the space when working at home. Some people might have a office, but some of us have work stations or corners.   I have a corner. Although, I don't have much room, I am able to stay fairly well organized. I have a shelf, a desk and a drawer – with a file cabinet in another room and this is all I need.

Most of the organizing is on the computer so I don't need a lot of outside room. I print out pertinent records and file them accordingly. I have a 4-story paper tray which holds all my "need now or soon" papers.   The shelf holds my printer, answering machine and phone.   And I also have a junk drawer (we all need one of those)!   ;-)   This works out with very few or no problems.

Although working at home does have some disadvantages, I would not want to give it up for anything. I love the freedom of it, the excitement of it, the pride of it, and all the wonderful people I have met.

If you feel you are a candidate for a home business or job, I say go for it, but I wish you much success in whichever path you choose!

#23

How Do You Measure Success?

When someone asks you if you are successful, how do you answer? How does one measure success?

You are a Mother and a housewife who decided to try something new, challenging and rewarding. So you start an online business. You work hard for 6 months and your income is just starting to trickle in. You are frustrated and close to giving up hope because you think you are a failure.

STOP! And think about that for awhile.

What exactly constitutes a failure in this business? Do you have to be making $5000 a month by this time to be a success? Who sets the standard for success and failure?

As for myself, when I first started Internet marketing I didn't even know how to turn on a computer! Getting as far as I am today, to me is a great success! Do not measure your success solely by how much money you make each month!

Here are a few things to think about when deciding if you are a success:

1. Do you enjoy what you do?

2. Have you made new friends and enjoyed relationships with lots of interesting new people?

3. Do you get personal satisfaction from working your business?

4. Is your family proud of you and are you, yourself proud of your accomplishments thus far?

5. Are you building a clean and honest reputation?

6. Are you being true to yourself and your customers?

7. Are you growing along with your business?

8. Are you more self-confident and sure of yourself and your capabilities?

9. Do you feel more in control of yourself and your life?

10. In general, are you happy about your business?

If you answered yes, to most or all of these questions, I believe you are success! Accomplishing all the above tasks are the first steps to building your online income. When you start from the bottom and build a business one day at a time, it will take time and if you are not making a lot of money after 6, 8, or 12 months, that does not make you a failure.

After the first steps fall into place and start taking effect, your income will grow and expand also. Do not expect to start making money the minute your website is up. There are many misleading ads and scammers out there that will tell you otherwise, but as long as you work at your business, build your reputation, and do not give up, your income will follow.

There are many ways to measure success. Do not feel that the amount of money you are making is the epitome of your success!

#24

Treat Yourself to a Mini-Vacation & Reduce Stress!

Most of us lead fairly hectic lives dealing with family, home, jobs, finances, etc. We could all use a little time to ourselves - i.e. a mini-vacation. There are several ways we can escape for our vacation.

Some of my favorites are listed below:

1. Nature Walk! Get out of the house and experience nature. Take a walk in the woods or through the park and note all the sounds of the birds and animals and even the wind. Close your eyes and let yourself get lost in the beautiful sounds of nature.

2. Exercise! Exercise is one of the best stress relievers there is. Walking, aerobics, dancing, or whatever form of exercise you choose has many more benefits also.

3. Read a Book! Escape to another time and place! When you are ready, come back to your world.

4. Call a Friend! A stimulating conversation with a friend can erase a lot of stress. Better yet, if you can, go visit them for awhile.

5. Soak in the Tub! Although this is not one of my favorites, I know it helps a lot of people. Let the water wash away all the tension and stress!

6. Exercise your Mind! Do some crossword puzzles, play some Mahjong, or solve some riddles. Exercising your mind can be surprisingly relaxing!

7. Sneak Away with your Spouse! Find a private spot anywhere in the house or outside. Take some time to really talk and just enjoy the pleasure of each other's company.

8. Travel the World! Go to a nice quiet spot and let your mind wander to anywhere in the world. Daydream the stress away. You should also be taking some nice, deep cleansing breaths.

9. Stretch the Stress Away! Even if it is only for 10-15 minutes. Walk around the house, stretch your muscles, do a few neck and back stretches. These can do wonders!

10. Just relax! Turn everything off, make yourself a cup of coffee, cocoa, or just plain water. Just sit in complete silence and watch the birds outside or put a cool cloth over your eyes. Let your mind go blank for awhile. Forget everything and just relax!

11. Have some fun! Put on some of your favorite music and dance around the house for awhile. Let loose and have some fun. Act goofy, crazy or waltz yourself to China. This helps get out some of the frustrations and pent up emotions that can cause stress!

Some of the above methods are great for reducing stress. If you have something that works better for you, by all means, try to do it everyday! We all need to take more mini-vacations!

#25

Make Mistakes -But Learn from Them!

If you are thinking about or have already started your own business, you probably know that you will make mistakes.   Don't let this dissuade you from your dreams or your passion.   We have all made them and will make more - no matter how experienced or how good we are at our business.

The difference between a good mistake and a bad mistake is whether or not you have learned from it.

Take some time to go over your mistake -

Why was it a mistake?
What can I do to prevent this type of mistake again?
How can I rectify this mistake?
What have I learned from this mistake?
How can I do this better next time?

I have made several mistakes over the years, especially when I was first starting out.   I made sure I realized the mistake, learned from the mistake and became stronger and more determined because of the mistake.

Some things you can do, however, to help reduce the number of mistakes you make are:

Research - Learn as much as you can about starting and running your own business. You do not want to go blindly into the business world.

Keep Learning - Don't think that your initial research will hold you over forever. The business world is constantly changing and you need to keep up with those changes.

When in Doubt, Find Out - You cannot guess your way to a successful business. When you have doubts about something, read up on it. Research and research some more.

Network - Get involved with message boards, email discussion groups and other networking communities. Learn from others who have made mistakes and have experienced what you are starting to experience. By learning from the mistakes of others, you can greatly reduce the number of mistakes you make.   ;-)

Experiment - Try different things until you find what is best for you and your business. Do not let yourself be pressured into doing things you know or "feel" are wrong.

I hope this article confirms your belief that we all make mistakes and it is not the end of the world. Just remember to learn from them, grow from them and become stronger from them!!

#26

Romance....Then & Now

Romance is something we should always hold on to. It keeps us young, happy, alive and energetic. Romance is not something you should wait until you have time for. It should be a continuing part of your life. There are many ways to keep the romance alive in your relationship. However, romance today may be a bit different than it was 50 years ago!!

Then: Leave a love note in your husband's lunchbox.
Now: Send your spouse a romantic email.

Then: Meet your husband at the door naked when he comes home from work.
Now: Make an appointment to actually be home at the same time!

Then: Have a candlelight dinner waiting for your husband when he comes home.
Now: Fax your spouse's secretary to have him/her meet you at a nice restaurant.

Then: Fill the house with beautiful fresh flowers!
Now: Go online and have flowers delivered to your spouse.

Then: Surprise your spouse with a romantic phone call.
Now: Leave a sexy message on your spouse's voicemail.

Then: Have a leisurely picnic in the park.
Now: Take your notebooks outside and have a quick sandwich.

Then: Stroll together on the beach.
Now: Put on the ocean channel and get on the treadmill together!

Then: Say "I love you" everyday.
Now: Say "I love you" everyday.

The point I am making with this is that love is love and no matter how busy we are or how hectic things get, we need to keep that love alive.

Take some time, slow down and enjoy each other. Life is short! Do not let it slip away without experiencing love, romance and fun everyday, not just on Valentine's Day!

****

Terri Seymour and her husband Terry offer a no-cost, non-MLM home business opportunity. They strive to help you build a successful home business. They also provide a website building service.

#27

Inexpensive Storage Ideas

Storage space is a problem for a lot of us. We tend to accumulate more stuff than we could ever hope to have room for. Before you throw everything out, get creative and find storage space in the least likely of places.

Use a chest or wooden box as a coffee table. Decorate to match your living room decor. These are great for storing blankets, books, pillows, magazines, etc.

Build a smaller version of the coffee table, add a cushion and use it as a footstool. Great for storing tapes, CDs, cards, etc.

Inexpensive plastic tubs can be used in kids' rooms as a toy chest, or storage for games, clothes, art supplies, etc. I have two stacked by my bed and they serve as a dresser for lesser worn clothes. Saves me tons of room in my closet!

Suitcases can be used for storage also. Stack a couple to double as a nightstand. Cover with pretty fabric for a coordinating look.

Put shelves above your doorways and windows. These shelves could be used for books, movies, pictures, collectibles and much more.

Baskets are a wonderful invention for home storage. Use them in the bathroom for cosmetics, toiletries, towels, etc. In the kitchen they can hold utensils, recipes, or food items. Try them for magazines, books, or movies in the living room or bedroom. In the kids' room they make great places for toys, books, video games. The possibilities are endless!

Use a file cabinet as a nightstand and/or end table. This is a great way to hide all your papers, bills, files, old magazines, etc.

Canning jars also make for good storage. They can be used for make-up, craft supplies, spices, pet food, small toys, etc.

Kids' rooms usually need a lot of storage for toys, games, art supplies, books, etc. Some stuff to use for storage could be inexpensive laundry baskets, decorated coffee cans, plastic shoe bags, and stackable plastic boxes in a variety of colors. Make your kid's room fun, easy for them to clean and interesting.

Take advantage of the space under your bed. Buy the under the bed plastic containers to store just about anything.

If you have an available corner or unused space, a dresser makes a great addition to your kitchen. The drawers are great for storing napkins, towels, utensils, foil/bags, odds and ends, etc. It can also double as a microwave stand!

Use your imagination and be creative. You do not have to follow "the rules" when it comes to decorating your own house! Do what you like and what works for you!

#28

What a Tangled Web We Weave........

The World Wide Web or www is a wonderful, inspiring, endless, fantastic place. They do call it a web for a reason - there are hundreds of thousands of websites all linked together out there. You want to be sure and get yours linked to plenty of those sites for a better position in the web.

When you are getting your link exchange campaign ready, keep these tips in mind:

1. Link to sites that are rich in content.

2. Choose sites that are complimentary to yours, example: if you have a site that sells pet supplies, link to sites that give info on how to care for pets, or where to get pets, etc.

3. Make sure your link text contains targeted keywords.

4. Stay away from link farms, which are sites that just have links of all kinds, good or bad, relevant or not.

5. You also want your site to be rich in content, so more sites will link to you.

6. Set up a main/category page for your links directory and then have each category have it s own page. You don't want just a jumbled mess of links.

7. Do not call you links page, links - call it a resource directory or something similar.

8. You could set up an ezine directory similar to your resource directory for even more web connections.

9. When you find a site you like, email the webmaster, using their name and tell them why you like their site.
Give them your url so they can take a look at your site.
Introduce yourself ask them to consider your site for an exchange.

To help save time, have a copy of this request saved on your desktop or in a email folder or where ever you prefer, so you can just open it up and make any changes and send.

I had a link exchange directory earlier on MOE and then decided to remove it (big mistake) because I was adding a paid home business directory.   Well, shortly thereafter, I noticed a drop in my traffic and in my sales. I am now building a bigger and better Resource Directory on MOE and on my new site as well.

So, let's get going on getting a good spot in this tangled web of sites. Good luck in your linking campaign!

#29

Search Engine Tips & Techniques

As you are building your site or getting your site built, you need to do as much as you can to ensure higher rankings in the search engines. There are a variety of little tips and techniques you can use to do this.

Meta tags & keywords - Meta tags are included in the <HEAD> section of your site and are read by the search engines. The two most important kind are "description" and "keywords." Description is a description of the content of your site and keywords is a list of keywords relevant to the page.

Site content- Make sure you match your site content with your meta tags. Also, keep updating your site content. Search engines love new content. Try adding articles to your site or doing a blog. Do NOT let your site get old and stale!

Blogging - A blog is basically a journal that is posted on a web site. A person who blogs is a blogger. Blogs are usually updated daily or every other day. Blogs can be used on personal or business websites. Blogs can draw a lot of targeted traffic to your site.

Site map - A site map is simply a page that lists all the links on your site. This makes it easy for the search engines to spider your site. A site map page is a good navigational tool for your visitors as well. It contains links to all important pages of your web site and it gives your visitors an overview of your web site structure all in one page.

Links page - Having a quality reciprocal links page can benefit your site in several ways. First of all, it gets your site listed in more places on the net which can bring you more traffic. More and more major search engines will rank your pages higher when there are more links to your site. Also, quality links can help the spiders find you more easily each week, therefore keeping you indexed longer and dropped less frequently.

Articles - Not only do you want to post relevant articles on your site, but writing and submitting them to other sites will help you as well. Posting new articles on your site will keep your content fresh and new so the spiders like your site. It will also keep your visitors coming back for more.

Using these techniques and others will greatly improve your rankings in the search engines and bring you more targeted traffic which in turn can increase your sales substantially!

30

How to Have Your Own Online Party!

Online parties can be a successful and fun way to build your home business. These parties are similar to home parties except that you do not have to pay a small fortune for refreshments and snacks! ;-)

You can have your party in a free or low cost chat room or you can have your party via email. Be sure and create a relaxed and fun atmosphere for your guests. We would recommend a chat room.

You can either recruit someone to host the party for you or you can be the host. There is also something called "Mystery Host Party". This is where you draw or randomly select a guest to be the "Mystery Host" and receive the host benefits.

You will need to schedule your party. We have found that during the week is best unless it is winter. Then weekends can be a good time also. Give yourself plenty of time to plan and send out invitations.

Plan your specials. You definitely want to have some items on special. Maybe some that ties in with your theme, if you have one. Give a 25% discount on certain items, but make sure you leave enough profit as well. You could also offer a small free gift with all orders over $25, for example.

When it is time to send out the invites, email groups and message boards can be a great place to start. Send out the invitations (follow guidelines on this). Also invite friends, neighbors, co-workers. Let everyone know they can bring a guest or two or however many they like.

Have each guest introduce themselves and tell (type) a little about themselves. This will help bring the guests together.

You also want to make sure you have some fun and interesting games to play. And of course, for each game you will need prizes. Below are some popular party games:

*Scavenger Hunt - make a list of several items and instruct your guests to find them on your site.

*Word Scramble - Pick about 10 words from your site and see who can get them all right in the least amount of time. Let your guests know the words come from your site/business.

*Trivia Questions - Write up a list of questions about your site/business.

There are many more fun, exciting games to play at your party!   Make up your own if you like as well.

You, of course, will also want to spend some time presenting your products. If you offer home decor items, share some tips and ideas on home decorating with your products. If you offer aromatherapy items, explain the benefits of your products. Make your presentation fun, informative and relaxed. Let the quests ask questions and always be clear and candid with your answers

The idea here is to relax, have fun, show your items and make new contacts/customers. If your guests have a good time and enjoy themselves, they will sure to come back to your next party! ;-)

#31

The "Not So Secret" Secrets of Success

Have you ever heard of the "secrets of success"? Many times people are trying to sell you these "secrets" for a very high price!   Well, in my five years of Internet marketing experience, I haven't learned any "secrets".

These so-called "secrets" are mostly common sense and hard work. We all know these "secrets". We just have to apply them and use them consistently.

"Secret" #1 - People

Dealing with people can be hard, but we all know we must be courteous and professional. You need to accept the fact that you cannot please everybody. When you come across one of these people you cannot please no matter what you do, just deal with them firmly, but courteously and professionally. **Not a "secret"!**

Seymour Products Motto -Treat people as you would like to be treated!

"Secret" #2 - Passion

We all know that we need to like we do in order to be really successful at it. If you are interested in pets do not start a business dealing with cars! ;-) Building an online business will take a lot of passion to get through the frustration, obstacles, and other difficulties. There will be many times when we will need our passion to get us through! **Not a "secret"!**

"Secret" #3 - Customer Service

Another "secret" is to treat the customer with respect and courtesy. It will not be easy to deal with difficult customers this way, but it can be done. I have worn down some of the nastiest customers by a continuing campaign of courtesy, politeness and professionalism!

Each time I dealt with this one lady, she was less and less rude and upset and more relaxed and easy to deal with. Eventually, she was thanking me and praising me for being so helpful and nice.   Don't be condescending and don't let yourself get upset.   Remain calm, yet be firm and respectful. **Not a "secret"!**

"Secret #4 - Promotion

To build a business, people must know that you and your business exist. Advertising, promotion and networking are how this is done. Set up a promotion schedule and stick with it. Be consistent. This may get tedious at times, but it must be done!

Write and submit articles, publish an ezine, get listed all over the web, do link exchanges, swap ezine ads, compile a free ebook for viral marketing, subscribe to announcement lists, visit message boards, get involved in discussion groups........there are hundreds of ways of promoting yourself and your online business! **Not a "secret"!**

"Secret" #5 - Hard Work

Despite what many people have said, it is not easy to "get rich overnight" and "making thousands a week, while doing nothing" just doesn't happen. To be successful you will need to work and work hard. This is where passion for your work comes in! **Not a "secret"!**

"Secret" #6 - Commitment

Expanding on the hard work "secret", you will need to make a commitment to success. You must be willing to make sacrifices and work long hours. This will not happen overnight....it could take years. Are you prepared for years of frustration, hard work, ups and downs, dealing with people (good and bad), rejections, and everything else that comes along with building a business? **Not a "secret"!**

"Secret" #7 - Pride

Take pride in your work. Your work and your business will be a reflection of you. Build your reputation for a solid foundation of success. Be true to yourself and your business. **Not a "secret"!**

"Secret" #8 - Goals

Be aware of what you want and how you want to get it. Do not go blindly into business without some planning of your goals and accomplishments. Use short term smaller goals to eventually reach your long term ultimate goal of success. **Not a "secret"!**

So we know in order to start and build a business, we must plan our goals, be prepared for the work and commitment of building that business, and that we must build a reputation of trust and professionalism.

I know we all knew that. It just helps to be reminded once in awhile! ;-)